One Thousand Stories About the Patchwork Blanket

Written By: **Ariana Espiritu**

Illustrated by: **Liliane Grenier**

An Original Playbook®

Presented in....

Playbook® Advantage Format

© 2014 PLAYBOOKS, INC, LAKE FOREST, CA. ALL RIGHTS RESERVED.

GLC 3-5
RS 2-5
Story Length: 3,167 Words

One Thousand Stories About the Patchwork Blanket

PUBLISHED BY PLAYBOOKS, INC.
d.b.a. Playbooks Reader's Theater

Copyright © 2014 by Playbooks, Inc., Lake Forest, CA.
All Rights Reserved.

ISBN 978-1-60476-096-5

The unique format of a Playbook® with character colorization and specialized readability levels is a proprietary method of book structure, writing, format, construction, re-construction, displaying and printing protected under U.S. Patent Nos. 6,683,611, 6,859,206, and 7,456,834 with additional patents pending. For information regarding licensing the rights to write, edit, construct, re-construct, display, print or publish any book in Playbook® format call 1-800-375-2926. No part of this publication may be reproduced in whole or in part, or stored in a retrieval system, or transmitted in any form or by any means, electronic, mechanical, photocopying, recording, or otherwise, without written permission of the publisher, except by a reviewer, who may quote brief passages in a review. For information regarding permission, call Playbooks, Inc. at 1-800-375-2926. This book is subject to the condition that it shall not, by way of trade or otherwise, be re-sold, hired out, or otherwise circulated without the publisher's prior consent in any form of binding or cover other than that in which it is published and without a similar condition including this condition being imposed on the subsequent purchaser. Performances of this story/script may be videotaped for school or library purposes.

Being a Star Makes Reading Fun™

Welcome to the world of Playbooks® and the beginning of a wonderful role-play reading adventure! Playbook® stories are presented in a unique and colorful format and are read out loud by several readers like a play, without memorization, props, or a stage. When you read a Playbook®, you and other readers bring the story to life and become the characters. As you read **your** part out loud, you will have fun expressing and acting like your character. You and the other readers will explore the story plot together and learn what will happen next. It's an exciting journey of discovery that pulls you into the story, and you'll want to read it out loud again and again!

HOW TO GET STARTED

Begin your reading adventure with the **Character Summary** here at the beginning of the book. **You'll notice right away that the words and sentences for each character appear in a different color here and throughout the book. This will make it easy to follow along and read your part with confidence and enthusiasm.**

It doesn't matter whether you are a beginning reader or an experienced reader; there is a part for everyone. The number of characters in the story may not match the number of readers in your group and that's okay. Readers can play more than one character role, or readers can share a role by taking turns.

Once your role has been assigned, you and the other readers will each read his or her character's summary out loud from his or her own copy of the book. The most experienced reader typically reads the narrator's role. **It's important for teachers and parents to refer to the Teacher or Parent Guide when assigning roles.**

Have fun bringing your character to life by bringing your voice up and down, speaking softly or loudly, changing your facial expressions, and moving your hands or body. Trying different voices or accents can also be lots of fun.

Sometimes you will see *black italicized text* inside parenthesis before or in the middle of sentences. **These are called "cues" and tell you how to read a sentence with expression.** For example, if the "cue" says *(with surprise),* speak the sentence with surprise in your voice! Cues are not read out loud.

MAKING THE MOST OF THE STORY

It's more fun to read the story out loud together with other readers the first time you read your role. It's exciting to discover the story in this way rather than each reader practicing his or her part alone first. As you get better with your role, you may want to change the way you express your character's personality, or you may want to switch roles with another reader. Be creative! When all your readers get comfortable with their roles, you may want to read the story in front of a friendly audience.

Reading out loud is so much fun that it's easy to forget about the other readers. **So be sure to read with good manners!** Here are some helpful hints. Stay quiet when other readers are reading. Follow along and keep up and be ready to read when it's your turn. Speak loudly and clearly so everyone can hear you. Stay in character for the whole story! Most importantly, enjoy your role-play reading experience. **You and your cast of characters are ready to begin your Playbook® adventure!**

FOR TEACHERS AND PARENTS

For specific guidance on implementing a Playbook® story in the classroom or in the home, download a FREE Teacher or Parent Guide at the following link.
http://www.readerstheater.com/teacherguide.pdf

It's important for students to be assigned a role they can read with success in front of their peers. A "Recommended Reader Assignment" chart that identifies the reading level for each story character is included in this story's group set. To print additional copies, visit www.readerstheater.com/rra.html and locate the story's title.

Being an active participant in a story spikes the reader's curiosity to learn more about the story's theme. Rewarding a child for exceptional effort and performance is an excellent practice for boosting a child's reading confidence. To download **FREE Award Certificates** to recognize star performers, visit www.readerstheater.com/awardcertificates.pdf.

Playbooks, Inc. also provides story-specific activity suggestions and worksheets to reinforce concepts and go beyond the story into the content areas of Language Arts, Math, Science, Social Studies, Art, Health, etc., as well as Character Development. Activities range in skill level and age-appropriateness, so the teacher or parent can choose activities that best suit the readers. Activities include comprehension quizzes, crossword puzzles, word search, vocabulary, discussion and writing prompts, story mapping, word problems, etc. To download FREE supplemental activity sheets for this and other stories, visit www.readerstheater.com/supplements.html.

Seeing children develop a passion for reading while working with the Playbook® format will be one of your greatest rewards.

Character Summary

Before beginning this story, it is helpful for each reader to read his/her character's summary aloud.

Holly

My name is Holly Hamwood, and I am a reporter from the *Big City Times*. I love to ask questions and get to the bottom of a juicy story. With my trusty notepad in hand, I know I'll find the truth about Sleepytown and the giant patchwork blanket!

River

I'm River. Ask me what's in my backpack, and I'll show you some of the coolest gadgets you've ever seen! That's because I made them myself. I'm an inventor, and I love learning and creating new things.

Clementine

Hey, there! My name is Clementine, and I have a twin brother who looks just like me. Above all, we love Sleepytown and the people who live in it. We plan all the events that go on here, and we love to have fun!

Character Summary

Before beginning this story, it is helpful for each reader to read his/her character's summary aloud.

Branden

Clementine's twin brother over here! My name is Branden. My favorite thing about Sleepytown is the big patchwork blanket, of course! My sister and I make sure everyone in town feels included no matter who they are.

Hiro

Hi, I'm Hiro. I love to bake things that remind me of Sleepytown *and* Japan. I make the best pies in town. Want to know why? Because they're filled with a one-of-a-kind surprise!

Mrs. Jan

Hello, I am one of the original residents of this little community. I am calm and serene … just like my favorite color, purple! I know the *real* story of Sleepytown and how its big patchwork blanket came to be. If the timing is right, I just might tell you!

Character Summary

Before beginning this story, it is helpful for each reader to read his/her character's summary aloud.

Small Parts -

Annie the Preschool Teacher *(same reader as Clementine)*

Bob the Mailman *(same reader as Branden)*

Narrator

As the narrator, I am the master storyteller! It's up to me to keep the story alive and engaging with each exciting detail. So, I must read everything with expression and excitement!

What is Cue Text? *Cue text tells readers HOW to read their lines. Cue text is shown in both italics and parentheses and appears before a line of dialogue. Cue text is not read aloud.*

Example: *(yelling)* Look out!

Narrator What is the best story you have ever heard? Did it have secret tunnels or talking cats? What about daring princesses and dancing tacos? Did it make you laugh or cry? As a reporter, Holly Hamwood has heard a lot of crazy tales, but nothing could have prepared her for Sleepytown and the biggest blanket in the world. Wait … you've never heard the story of the world's largest blanket?

It all began when the *Big City Times* sent Holly Hamwood to a little place called Sleepytown. Rumor had it that Sleepytown was home to an exceptionally big blanket and that a particular world record could be broken at the town's upcoming community event. Notepad in hand, Holly hit the streets of that tiny town where she bumped into a little girl with big ideas.

Holly Hi there! I'm Holly Hamwood, reporter for the *Big City Times*. I'm a little lost.

Narrator	Holly pulled out her notepad and looked at it with squinty eyes.
Holly	Do you happen to know where I can find a very big blanket?
River	Oh, a reporter, huh? Yeah, I know the blanket you're talking about, everyone does, but wouldn't you be much more interested in writing about a walkie-talkie that flies?!
Narrator	River threw her walkie-talkie up into the air. Right before it hit the ground, helicopter propellers sprung out from its top, and it hovered up to Holly's face. Holly's mouth was wide open in shock.

River	I made this myself. It works, I talk to my friends on it all the time. It's waterproof and practically unbreakable. It also has a clip to attach to your back pocket.
Narrator	She quickly opened the zipper of her backpack.
River	I have hundreds more like it if you want to buy one!
Holly	*(impressed)* Wow! That's amazing!
Narrator	Holly was fascinated by the fluttering object, but she shook her head as she regained focus on the task at hand.
Holly	*(apologetic)* I'm sorry, kid. That's not what I'm here for. Can you please tell me where I can find the blanket?
Narrator	Just then, a jolly-looking man came winding down the path. He waved cheerfully and called out to River.
Hiro	River! How is it going today?
River	Hi, Hiro! Well, I haven't sold any walkie-talkies today yet, but I've just improved the design. By the way, we have a visitor!
Hiro	Hi, there.

Holly	Nice to meet you. I'm Holly from the *Big City Times.*
River	She was just asking me about the blanket.
Holly	Yes, can you tell me where it is?
Hiro	*(pointing behind him)* Sure, it's up the hill.
River	I can walk you over there if that's what you *really* want to write your story about.
Holly	Great! Thanks so much.
Narrator	**Holly jotted down a few words in her trusty notepad.**
Holly	*(matter-of-factly)* So, what's your name?
Holly	What can you tell me about this blanket that's been stirring up such a buzz?
River	My name is River, and I am an inventor of awesome stuff!
Hiro	It is true! She comes up with the best things.
River	I've lived in Sleepytown all my life. That old blanket has been around ever since I can remember.
Narrator	**Holly began scribbling rapidly.**

Narrator	Every now and then, she looked up excitedly at her young interviewee.
River	Every year, each family in Sleepytown makes a new patch for the blanket. The new patches are stitched to the blanket on Patch Day. Patch Day is tomorrow, so you're just in time.
Hiro	That's right! It is good you are here!
River	This year, the rumors say that the new patches will break a world record. *(sarcastically)* But if you ask me, it sets the record for the most boring thing in the world.
Hiro	I don't think it's boring. I love Patch Day.
Holly	*(in disbelief)* So, you're not excited about it, River?
River	I like new, shiny things. That blanket is old and smells kind of funny. See for yourself and follow me.
Hiro	I am going that way, too. I am glad to help our new friend.
Narrator	They climbed a steep hill and just over the top stretched the biggest blanket Holly had ever seen.

Narrator	Patches stitched together spanned as far as the eye could see, and there were people everywhere.
Holly	Wow! Now that's a blanket!
Narrator	Kids ran over the top of the blanket, laughing and rolling on its multi-patterned surface. Holly stood frozen in awe. She was surprised to see that River, however, just looked bored.
Holly	Wow. I've never seen anything quite like this. It seems like the entire town is here.
Hiro	Everyone *is* here.
River	*(still bored)* Yeah, we all hang out around the blanket before Patch Day to look at the patches from last year and talk about the new ones we made for this year.
Holly	So, what is the story behind this amazing patchwork blanket?
Narrator	Uninterested, River shrugged, indicating that she didn't know. By now, her nose was deep into her gadget, and she was tinkering with its helicopter wings. It was then that a whirling, red Frisbee smacked the back of Holly's head.

Holly	*(surprised)* Ouch! What in the world was that?
Narrator	A man and a woman quickly approached. They both had bright red hair, big grins, and skipped as they walked. The woman ran closer and picked up the Frisbee while the man nervously twisted his mustache.
Clementine	So sorry about that!
Branden	Hi, River. Hi, Hiro. Who's your friend?
Holly	Hello, I'm Holly Hamwood, reporter from the *Big City Times*.
River	This is Clementine, and her brother, Branden, our town's community organizers.
Branden	*(with a huge smile)* That means we make sure that everyone in the community gets together from time to time.
Clementine	We hold meetings in the town square and plan events like hot dog eating contests and concerts in the park.
Hiro	They started Patch Day.
Holly	There wasn't always a Patch Day?
Clementine	Nope.

Clementine	Before we came along, not just anyone was allowed to add patches to the blanket. It was only for those who had lived here for generations, and there were only a few of those families still living here.
Branden	The blanket is such a big part of our town, we wanted everyone to be a part of it.
Hiro	Newcomers and all!
Narrator	River looked up.
River	*(curiously)* Hmm, I actually didn't know that.
Branden	*(pointing)* See where the blanket starts looking different?
Narrator	Holly turned her head towards the part of the blanket where Branden pointed. She saw a sea of old grey and white patches make way for bright reds, yellows, purples, and oranges.
Hiro	The old parts all look the same. The new parts are all different colors!
Branden	*(cheerful)* You can tell which patches were added after Patch Day began.

Branden — Now, no matter who you are or where you come from, you can be a part of our town.

Clementine — Now, all our citizens can share the day with their children, and their children will share it with their children. You know what I'm saying. It's a tradition now, for the whole town.

River — What's a tradition?

Holly	A tradition is a practice or belief that is passed down from generation to generation.
Hiro	Tradition is very important! My family has many traditions.
Holly	Looks like celebrating Patch Day has become a pretty sweet tradition!
Clementine	It gets even sweeter! Wait until you try a Patch Day Pie. We were just heading out to your bakery, Hiro, to check up on the pies for tomorrow. Are you going back there soon?
Hiro	Yes, I am finished here.
Branden	Would you like to join us, Miss Hamwood?
Holly	Absolutely!
Narrator	With pen and paper in hand, Holly jumped to follow them. River decided to tag along. She could never turn down a sweet treat, and the stories about Patch Day were starting to get very interesting. They didn't go very far.

Narrator	**The bakery was exactly five hops and two skips away from the patchwork blanket, the only shop on the hill. Hiro donned his chef hat as they walked in.**
Hiro	Here we are!
Clementine	*(sniffing and smiling)* One of my favorite places! So how are our pies doing?
Hiro	All ready for the big day! Please have a taste.
Narrator	**Clementine, Branden, and River all stepped aside so that Holly could take her first bite of Patch Day Pie.**
Holly	Mmm, this is delicious! It's warm, gooey, sweet, and chewy. It's an amazing combination.
Branden	*(laughing)* It's not like any pie you have ever tried, right?
Holly	No, it's not. It's quite unique.
Hiro	That is because all Patch Day pies are filled with my special mochi.
Branden	Mochi is a traditional dessert in Japan.
Hiro	Yes, but this is my family's *secret recipe*. I grew up in Japan.

River   I didn't know that.

Hiro   My grandmother taught me how to make this special mochi just like her grandmother taught her!

River   Hiro's pies have always been my favorite part of Patch Day.

Holly   How did you think of putting mochi into a pie?

Hiro   When I moved to Sleepytown many years ago, I missed home. I missed my family and how we cooked together.

Clementine   Hiro always says his very favorite thing to make with his family was mochi.

Holly So it was a special tradition for you?

Hiro Yes. When I opened up this store here, I wanted to make something new from both my life in Sleepytown and my life in Japan.

River *(trying to hide her excitement)* So how did it become Patch Day Pie?

Hiro The first time I made a pie filled with mochi was the same day as the first Patch Day.

Clementine When my brother and I came into this store to tell Hiro about our new Patch Day celebration, we smelled the pies and had to try some.

Branden We convinced the town committee to buy fifty pies that day and served them to all the people who showed up at the first Patch Day.

Clementine Hiro makes a patch for the blanket every year just like the rest of us, but he also has this very special job to do.

Hiro I make Patch Day Pie every year. It has become almost *a part of* the blanket.

Branden *(joking)* The part that tastes the best.

River	So that's why we eat Patch Day Pie every year. It's a tradition!
Holly	So Patch Day became a tradition, and so did Patch Day Pie through Hiro's special family recipe.
Narrator	Just then, River's walkie-talkie started buzzing and whirling around.
Holly	What was that?
Branden	It doesn't sound good.
River	I'm not sure. It's never done this before. Hey, get back here!
Narrator	The gadget flew above all of their heads, letting out a loud siren and a flashing red light. Then, across the screen, in bold letters, blinked: "WARNING: STORM ALERT!"
Hiro	What? It's such a sunny day out.
River	Not anymore. Look outside!
Narrator	Outside the tiny bakery, dark clouds were forming. They stepped out to see raindrops the size of golf balls falling from the sky.

Clementine	This could be the worst storm Sleepytown has ever seen! Why does this have to happen today?
Holly	*(pointing)* Oh, no! Look, the whole town is going to get caught in this!
Narrator	Down the hill, the rain had already formed rushing rivers in the streets of the town. Luckily, everyone in Sleepytown was on the hill getting ready for Patch Day, but now they were all stranded. They tried running down the hill for shelter but stopped when they saw the water rushing up towards the base of the hill. Everyone was soaking wet.

Hiro	Everyone, please get inside!
River	I don't think we can all fit in your bakery!
Narrator	River was right. The bakery could fit ten adults at most, and the entire town was seeking a dry place.
Holly	Well, we can't all stand here in the rain forever!
Hiro	It's raining even harder.
Clementine	It doesn't look like this storm is giving up any time soon.
Narrator	River began unloading the sea of gadgets from her backpack and handing them out to everyone nearby.
River	I have an idea! Please pass these out! There's a green "on" button at the top of each walkie-talkie, everyone press the button and attach it with the clip to a piece of the blanket.
Narrator	The walkie-talkies quickly made their way around the crowd until almost everyone in town was holding one in their hands. They all began clipping them to the edges of the blanket. The rain fell harder.

Narrator	River studied her own master gadget with its puzzle of buttons.
River	*(thinking)* Now, if I just turn all their propellers on….
Branden	The blanket!
Clementine	It's lifting!
Narrator	Slowly the blanket started to rise, fighting against the falling raindrops. Everyone watched and waited. The blanket lifted higher and higher.
Holly	Everyone, get underneath the patchwork blanket!
Narrator	People gathered under the blanket. Some were pacing, looking for their families, or yelling. One person in the crowd stood out. An old woman was sitting cross-legged in the crowd with a peaceful smile on her face. River recognized her right away.
River	Mrs. Jan. What are you doing sitting on the ground like that? Why are you smiling? This is a disaster!
Mrs. Jan	This reminds me of the old days when the blanket was new.

Hiro	You were there when it was first made?
Mrs. Jan	*(calm)* Yes. See how the patches are made with thick leather and canvas? That's so rain and snow couldn't soak through. The blanket didn't start out as a blanket. At first, it was a tent.
All Readers	A tent?!
Narrator	Mrs. Jan nodded. Everyone under the blanket was watching and listening to her words.
Holly	Can you tell us about the tent?
Mrs. Jan	A long, long time ago, when I was just a little girl, Sleepytown wasn't called Sleepytown. It's name was Storytown.

Mrs. Jan	That's because every night, everyone in the town would gather together on this hill and tell stories.
Clementine	I didn't know that.
Branden	Neither did I.
Mrs. Jan	They would tell stories about anything and everything! We built a small tent so we could have storytime, no matter the weather.
Holly	I see, very interesting.
Mrs. Jan	Soon, more and more people moved to Storytown and wanted to tell their own stories. When they did, they would get to add a patch to the tent to help make it larger.
Holly	So there could be a story behind every patch!
Mrs. Jan	Yes, and so our little tent grew bigger and bigger.
Holly	This is perfect! It's just the sort of story I want to bring to the *Big City Times*! *(talking quickly to herself)* A story tent tradition, a patch for every story, became a patchwork blanket, Patch Day, Patch Day Pie….

Narrator	Holly was furiously writing in her notebook, her eyes alight with the excitement of the developing story to report.
Hiro	So this rain just makes our tradition even better!
River	But Mrs. Jan, then what happened? Why did Storytown become Sleepytown?
Mrs. Jan	*(sadly)* People began to fight about who got to tell their stories. Everyone wanted to be a storyteller, and no one wanted to listen. So, some people left and the people who stayed just stopped the tradition.
Holly	What, they banned storytelling?
Mrs. Jan	The townspeople wanted to have peace even if that meant getting rid of a tradition. They took down the tent and began to tell newcomers it was a blanket.
Branden	And they didn't let people add patches anymore.
Mrs. Jan	That's right, and they renamed our town.
Clementine	So that's why we're called Sleepytown ... because of the blanket.

Mrs. Jan	Yes, but see how the blanket became its own tradition? Sometimes traditions are passed down exactly as they are, and sometimes they are changed and even made new.
Branden	Like how Clementine and I started Patch Day?
Mrs. Jan	Yes!
Hiro	Like my Patch Day Pie filled with mochi?
Mrs. Jan	Exactly like that.
Hiro	Did someone say pie? Hey, does anybody want some?
River	*(laughing)* I think we all do!
Narrator	Hiro had snuck some slices of pie when they were racing out of the bakery. The townspeople laughed and cheered and took large helpings of pie. Soon, people began telling their own stories about the patchwork blanket.
Annie - Teacher	*(pointing)* I did my first cart-wheel over that patch right there.

Bob - Mailman	I wrote, "Will you marry me," on a patch years ago! *(beaming with a smile)* She said, "yes."
Holly	*(swooning)* Aww, how romantic.
Narrator	The rain fell heavy and loud, but the stories were even louder as people enjoyed being under the blanket together. The rain finally stopped, and people continued to tell stories as they walked home. The next morning, it was Patch Day! The town buzzed with preparations.
River	Do you think we're going to beat the world record?
Hiro	How many new patches do we need?
Branden	The record is 999 patches. Our blanket has 900 patches already.
Clementine	We just need 100 more to make 1,000 patches!
Narrator	Holly counted as the families in Sleepytown began stitching their new patches onto the blanket. After what seemed like forever, the last few patches were sewn on.

Holly	*(counting)* Ninety-six, ninety-seven, ninety-eight, ninety-nine. That's it? You're one patch short.
River	I think that was the last patch we have.
Clementine	*(grinning)* No, it's not. There's one more to be made … by you, Ms. Hamwood!
Narrator	Clementine pulled out a large leather and canvas square. Branden plopped all different colors of paint by Holly's feet.
Clementine	You're part of our town now, too, because you're going to tell our story.
River	How are you going to paint your patch?
Holly	I'm not much of an artist. But let me see.
Narrator	Holly grinned and stuck her hand into one of the tubs of paint. She placed a big sticky handprint in the middle of the patch.
Holly	Now, I want you all to put your handprints on, too!
Narrator	Once the little group was done placing their prints on the patch. The canvas reflected a rainbow of hands of all sizes. Once it dried, River and old Mrs. Jan began to stitch it on. It was a beautiful addition to the patchwork blanket.

River	That makes 1,000 patches!
Narrator	The patchwork blanket beat the world record and became the biggest blanket in the world.
Branden	It also became the biggest tent in the world! Now, every weekend the patchwork blanket is lifted and transformed into a tent so that the people of our town can tell stories underneath.
Clementine	Yes, they take turns telling stories of all the patches they can remember.

Holly	So, eventually, 1,000 stories will be told, one for each patch.
River	So the story of our big, old, smelly blanket is cooler than I thought.
Holly	I think how the Patchwork Blanket became to be what it is today is a story worth telling over a thousand times!
River	Me, too!

THE END

www.ingramcontent.com/pod-product-compliance
Lightning Source LLC
Chambersburg PA
CBHW061806070526
44586CB00023B/2736